RITE

OF

PASSAGE

An Honorman's Guide to Marine Recruit Training

Kurt Jeter

Series Honor Graduate

3rd RTBN, I Company, Parris Island, SC

United States Marine Corps

To my wife, Tricia. Thank you for being a friend. And to Kristin and Jacob, thank you for being such wonderful children.

"Some people spend an entire lifetime wondering if they made a difference in the world. But, the Marines don't have that problem."
—Ronald Reagan, U.S. President; 1985

Table of Contents

Introduction

IF YOU'RE READING this now, chances are that you're seriously considering enlisting into *"The World's Finest Fighting Force,"* the United States Marine Corps. If so, I commend you. The defense of the United States and our freedoms is the duty and privilege of every citizen, yet few follow that call of duty or exercise that privilege. You're very special. If you weren't, you wouldn't be considering what you're considering now. It takes a special breed of man or woman to even *consider* becoming a Marine.

Since its inception on 10 November, 1775 in a little Philadelphia bar known as *Tun Tavern,* the Marine Corps has had a proud tradition of outstanding service to our country in times of peace as well as in times of war. Without question, *United States Marine Corps Recruit Training* is far more challenging—both mentally and physically— than the basic training programs of any of the other armed services. To voluntarily enlist in this elite military organization demonstrates one's patriotism and loyalty to the United States of America in a way that few acts can.

As a former Parris Island, 3rd Battalion Series Honor Graduate, or *Honorman* (I graduated number 1 of 240 recruits), my call of duty now is to prepare you for the greatest challenge you'll ever face— becoming a United States Marine. Not just anyone can become a Marine. The Marine Corps is the only branch of the U.S. Armed Services where one has to *earn* the title rather than just *sign up.* Many who attempt it won't make it. The *"few"* in the saying, *"The few, the proud, the Marines"* is accurately descriptive. When I attended recruit training, only a small percentage of the recruits who began with my platoon graduated with my platoon. The rest of the recruits were either "recycled" back to attempt their failed challenges again, thereby extending their graduation date, or were discharged, and never had the opportunity to claim the title, *Marine.* In hindsight, it's clear to me that those who failed to make it did so because they weren't *prepared* to make it.

In my book, *"Rite of Passage, An Honorman's Guide to Marine Recruit Training,"* I've attempted to provide you with more than just a "by the numbers" outline of Recruit Training requirements. Anyone can find that information just about anywhere online. In stark contrast to the "generic" Recruit Training guide, I've endeavored to help you develop the necessary *mindset* to not only *prepare* for the challenge of Recruit Training, but to *master* it. After all, being a Marine is not just about wearing the uniform. *It's a state of mind.*

To those of you who have begun your journey to follow your calling to become a United States Marine, I wish you the best, and Godspeed.

—Kurt Jeter, Panama City Beach, Florida
2016

Chapter 1: Enlistment Preparation

I REMEMBER GRADUATION Day at Parris Island like it was yesterday. On the Parade Deck, four Marine platoons dressed in khaki and green stood rigidly behind me at the position of attention, their heads and eyes steadfastly focused frontward. Their jaws were clenched and their backs were straight. An aura of dignity emanated from each and every graduate like rays from the sun. Parents, family, and friends shed tears from the wave of pride that flooded over from the Parade Deck into the bleachers. Fathers stood tall as if they themselves had just earned the title, *Marine.*

In front of this sea of khaki and green, I and three other Marines stood as resolute as our platoons, but were arrayed in *Dress Blues.* The four of us had earned the title, *"Platoon Honor Graduate."* We had also earned the right to receive and wear the Marine Corps' dress uniform during our graduation ceremony. Of the four Platoon Honor Graduates, I alone had earned the title, *"Series Honor Graduate."* This meant that I had not only completed Marine Corps Recruit Training, but that I would graduate number one of the 239 other men who would soon graduate with me. This also meant that I would have the privilege of meeting the Commanding General of Parris Island, Major General Joseph P. Hoar, who would present me with the *Leatherneck Award* and *Navy League Outstanding Recruit Award.*

Sometime during the latter part of the hour-long Graduation Ceremony, Major General Hoar left-faced in front of me and came to the position of attention. As we were taught, I immediately rendered a hand salute. The General returned my salute, we each dropped our arms to our sides, and with a look of pride the General stared me square in the eyes and said, *"Marine, I bet you're about ready to get off of this island."* Without hesitation, and proud to now be called a *Marine* rather than a *recruit,* I responded sternly, *"Sir no sir, I kinda like it here."* Silently, the General's rugged countenance morphed into an expression of satisfaction. He knew that his *Drill*

Instructors, or *DIs* as they're known, had successfully molded another highly motivated Marine out of the *"nasty stinkin' civilian"* that had arrived there three-and-a-half months earlier. He was very satisfied, and I was glad of it.

The Marine Corps' physical requirements are by far the most demanding of any of the U.S. Armed Services. Therefore, if you're serious about becoming a Marine, your first area of focus should be physical preparation. I enlisted in August under the *DEP,* or *Delayed Entry Program,* with a departure date of the following February. Not long after enlisting, my recruiter explained to me the physical requirements to become a Marine, and I decided that I better get my butt in gear. This gave me about six months to prepare for the Marine Corps' *Physical Fitness Test,* or *PFT.*

Although there are "minimum standards" for passing the PFT, I couldn't begin to tell you what they are. You shouldn't worry about them either. The Marine Corp isn't looking for someone who'll settle for just getting by. Instead, when I began preparing for the PFT, I used what I call the *Aim High Principle,* and set my sights on a perfect score of 300. It's the same principle as elevating the barrel of your rifle when you want to reach downrange farther—you aim high. Don't sell yourself short. If you set 300 as your goal, train for a 300, then you'll be amazed at your score when you take your *IST,* or *Initial Strength Test* shortly after arriving at Recruit Training. Remember, there's no limit to what you can achieve when you set goals for yourself that are reasonably higher than the "average" person's goals.

A perfect PFT score of 300 for a male would be to complete 20 consecutive strict-form (no kipping) pullups before dropping from the bar, perform 100 legal crunches (sit-ups) in two minutes, and run three miles in eighteen minutes or less. The same 300 score for a female would consist of a 70-second flexed-arm hang, 100 legal crunches, and a three-mile run completed in twenty-one minutes or less. Your local Marine

Recruiter will gladly help you in determining the correct form for these exercises.

The pullup portion of the PFT has always been considered the most difficult, so if you're having trouble repping them out, I highly recommend that you begin the *"Armstrong Pullup Program"* as soon as possible. You can find information on this program at *armstrongpullupprogram.com.* Users of the Armstrong Program claim to have achieved remarkable results in only 6-8 weeks. Whether or not you utilize the program, you'll be proud to know that it was created by Lieutenant Colonel Charles L. Armstrong—a hard-charging, highly motivated U.S. Marine.

Weight training was also a plus for me. A stronger Marine is a better Marine. I trained like an animal for six months, got my bench press up to 405 pounds at a body-weight of 176, and as a result, I mastered every physical challenge Recruit Training threw at me.

Keep in mind though, that although weight-training was certainly beneficial, I believe the physical strength I carried with me to Recruit Training resulted from the development of a *mindset* that was conducive to, and parallel with, that of the Marine Corps. Simply put, I adopted the mindset of a Marine as much as possible *before* Recruit Training, so that when I arrived there, I would look like, act like, think like, and believe like a Marine, thereby assuring myself (and my superiors) that I would eventually *become* a Marine. Essentially, I *became* a Marine in order to *become* a Marine.

That may sound strange, but Hollywood actors successfully "mimic" characters they portray by diligently studying about the characters and by spending time with them. I suggest that you read as much as possible about the Marine Corps, and spend as much time as you can with Marines. For example, set aside one day per week that you'll spend doing nothing but hanging out at your local Marine Recruiting Station, talking with Recruiters and reading Marine Corps literature.

Next, you'll want to ensure that you're going to spend your career as a Marine doing what you love. Although every Marine is a basic *Rifleman,* each individual Marine is assigned an *MOS,* or a *Military Occupational Specialty.* An MOS is nothing more than the military term for a job. A good way to get the job of your choice in the Corps is to score well on the *ASVAB,* or *Armed Services Vocational Aptitude Battery* test. A good score on the ASVAB ensures that you'll have a "bargaining chip" when it comes time to find out what jobs are available and for which of the available jobs you qualify.

There are many resources online to assist you with studying for the ASVAB. I took ASVAB practice tests over and over until I had the content virtually memorized. I also went out of my way to eat "brain food" the week before I actually sat for the ASVAB test, and ended up with a score of 96 out of a possible 99. Some good examples of memory-enhancing brain foods include blueberries, wild salmon, lots of nuts and seeds, and avocados. You'll also want to get plenty of sleep, especially during the several nights before the test. A no-brainer is to abstain from alcohol consumption, which burns up vital nutrients in the body. Remember, I did well not because I'm any stronger or smarter than the next guy, but rather because I worked harder than most by *preparing* to do well.

Not only are the physical and mental requirements demanding, but recruits are required to learn and memorize an enormous amount of information. In order to arrive at Recruit Training prepared, I would suggest that you begin the memorization of some of this relevant information as soon as possible. Some examples of things you'll need to know are *Marine Corps Rank Structure,* the *11 General Orders for a Sentry, USMC Core Values,* the Marine's *Code of Conduct,* and the *Marine Corps Hymn.* Additionally, you'll learn and be tested on a great deal of Marine Corps history, such as the *Battle of Iwo Jima,* and other significant Marine Corps historical events. Since *close-order drill* will start almost immediately upon your arrival at Recruit Training, you'll also want to study basic drill movements such as the *position of attention* and *about face.*

Last but certainly not least, you'll want to prepare yourself *spiritually.* Since 1883, the motto of the Marine Corps has been *Semper fidelis, or Semper fi* for short. In Latin, the term means *Always faithful.* Since its adoption by the Marine Corps, *Semper fi* to a Marine has meant *Always faithful to God, Corps, and country*—in that order. Contrary to what those "politically correct" Chiefs of Staff would have you believe, God's role in the Marine Corps always has been, and always will be, paramount. Even your enlistment oath will conclude with the words *"So help me God."* Moreover, you'll find out how important God is if you ever find yourself in a precarious combat situation. You know the old saying, *"There are no atheists in foxholes."*

When I enlisted, I understood that once I accepted the challenge I would become a part of something much greater than myself. Consequently, I reasoned that if I wanted to succeed, and remain unscathed while doing it, then I would need to call on something much greater than myself to empower and protect me. That something for me was the God of the Bible, our Creator. The God who came to earth to habitate with his creation in the form of Jesus Christ. The same God that American leaders from George Washington to George Bush have prayed to since our country's beginning.

Why this God, you may ask? Because unquestionably, Christianity provided the breath of life that animated our great nation in its infancy. Our U.S. Supreme Court said so in 1892, in the case of *"Church of Holy Trinity v. United States"* (143 U.S. 457). In that case the Court stated, *"This is a religious people...this is a Christian nation."* Knowing this, it just didn't make sense to me to put my faith in any other God (or no God) other than the God of the nation that I took an oath to protect and defend. To have done anything different would be like playing in the Super Bowl for one team, and getting instruction on play-calling from the coach of the opposing team (or no coach at all).

If and when you do enlist into the Marine Corps, you'll be known as a *Poolee*. Once you arrive at a Marine Base for Recruit Training, you'll then be known as a *recruit*. All Marine Corps recruits, whether they opt to serve active duty or reserves, are required to undergo Marine Corps Recruit Training at an *MCRD,* or *Marine Corps Recruit Depot.*

There are two MCRDs. Both are located in *CONUS,* or in the *Continental United States.* One is located at Parris Island, South Carolina, the other at San Diego, California. I've served at both; Parris Island as a Marine recruit, and San Diego as a Marine. Other than being on opposite sides of the country (and better weather for the *"Hollywood Marines"*), both training facilities are equally formidable. As one would expect, I'm partial to Parris Island for obvious reasons.

MCRD San Diego's main mission is the initial training of enlisted male recruits living west of the Mississippi River (except Louisiana and including parts of Illinois, Indiana, Wisconsin, and Michigan), while

MCRD Parris Island's is to train enlisted male recruits who live east of the Mississippi, as well as all female recruits. However, male recruits who live west of the Mississippi River may train at MCRD Parris Island by special request, which speaks volumes of the *esprit de corps* that exists there. Once you've made the commitment and prepared yourself to become a Marine, your final decision should be to decide where you want to undergo Recruit Training—San Diego or Parris Island.

After you've mastered the PFT and ASVAB, memorized some basic Marine Corps knowledge, strengthened yourself spiritually, and decided which MCRD you'd like to attend, you'll need to visit your local recruiter and begin the enlistment process. Before you sign on the dotted line, make sure your enlistment contract contains any special provisions concerning your choice of MCRDs and Occupational Specialties. Without those contractual guarantees, you'll go where they send you no matter what the recruiter promises you. A good rule of thumb to remember is to assume that if your recruiter's mouth is moving, he or she is probably lying, so make sure everything you're promised is in writing. This is especially important concerning your MOS. Without a job guarantee, you may find yourself proudly graduating as a U.S. Marine, then proudly cleaning porta johns for the next four years.

Ignorantly, I enlisted with no prior knowledge of the requirements of the Marine Corps, and no promise of a job—even though I had a 96 ASVAB score. Once I signed the contract, my enlistment was categorized as *Open Contract with No Guarantees.* What allowed me to receive a great education and a great job was the fact that I graduated *Series Honor Graduate.* Along with the tangible awards presented to me for graduating at the top of my class, I earned a *Meritorious Promotion* to Private First Class and the job of my choice. To graduate Honorman was a particularly arduous task, but once I learned of the Recruit Training requirements, and once I discovered that I had been duped by my Recruiter and had no job guarantee, I felt I had no choice but to master the requirements of Recruit Training in order to get a good job. Unfortunately, it was *after* I enlisted that I figured all of this out. By reading the information in this guidebook, you'll be able to know these things *before* you enlist and report for duty. By applying this knowledge, you'll be able to possess and maintain an invaluable advantage over your fellow recruits while undergoing an extremely competition-oriented enlistment process and Recruit Training.

Once you've enlisted and your *ship date* arrives, or the day you'll *ship out* for MCRD, you'll meet up with your recruiter at your local Recruiting Station, and hop on a van to your regional *MEPS,* or *Military Entrance Processing Station.* More than likely, this will be the same MEPS where you completed your enlistment processing. When you arrive at MEPS you'll be surrounded by a host of poolees, but you'll notice that only a handful of them will have chosen to enlist into the Marine Corps. If your final trip to MEPS is like mine was, *other Service* poolees will congratulate you for having the courage to enlist in the Marine Corps and some will admit to you that they couldn't manifest the courage to do it if their lives depended on it. If you're like me, you'll wonder whether or not you should be proud, or scared shitless.

Once you're done at MEPS, you'll then commute by plane or bus from MEPS to MCRD. During the ride, you'll need to be on your best behavior. Sleep if you can—you'll need it—and don't feed into any foolishness from other poolees who happen to forget who they are and where they're headed. Stay focused, stay motivated, and soon you'll be stepping out onto those famous yellow footprints of MCRD, well on your way to becoming a United States Marine.

Chapter 2: Receiving

RECEIVING BEGAN FOR me with an incident that I'll always remember. It occurred just after we arrived at MCRD while the Drill Instructors were herding us off of the bus and onto the yellow footprints. Although most of us were stunned by the cyclone of screaming and flailing Drill Instructors who "greeted" us, one recruit who swaggered off of the bus seemed to think the process was funny, and maintained a smirk on his face as we formed up. Suddenly, seemingly out of nowhere, a Drill Instructor met the smiling recruit chest to chest and began screaming,

"WHAT IN THE FUCK DO YOU THINK IS SO GOD DAMNED FUNNY?"

A dumbfounded look quickly replaced the recruit's smirk.

"LET ME TELL YOU ONE THING MAGGOT," the Instructor raged.

"I JUST LOST EVERY GODDAMNED FRIEND I HAD IN THIS WORLD, AND THERE

AIN'T A MOTHERFUCKING THING FUNNY TO ME!"

The recruit stood frozen and silent. His smile quickly vanished. After a brief ass-chewing, the recruit was finally allowed to step onto the yellow footprints and proceed with his indoctrination. That night, we all learned that the DI had been attached to 1st Battalion 8th Marines (1/8) prior to reporting for duty as a Drill Instructor. 1/8 was the infantry unit that had lost 220 Marines in the 1983 Beirut, Lebanon barracks bombing, and the Drill Instructor had been right in the middle of it when it happened. Reality had just slapped us all square in the face, and to this day I still feel guilty when I smile.

If you've made it through the enlistment process and are on the bus, then you're *eligible* to become a Marine. Proving that you're *capable* of becoming a Marine begins the moment you step off. Once you're ushered off of the bus into the darkness and onto the yellow footprints, you'll no longer be considered a civilian. You'll now be the "property" of the U.S.

Government. After getting your first introduction to a real-life Marine Corps Drill Instructor, you'll be introduced by him or her to the *UCMJ*, or the *Uniform Code of Military Justice*. These are the laws of the military, and special emphasis will be placed on three of the UCMJ's articles:

Article 86 will prohibit you from going *AWOL,* or *Absent without Leave*. These days AWOL is better known as *UA*, which stands for *unauthorized absence*. Being late for work or missing a medical appointment can be considered an unauthorized absence.

Next will be Article 91, which will prohibit you from disobeying a lawful order from your Drill Instructor or any other *Non-commissioned officer (NCO),* petty officer, or warrant officer. Remember, everything you'll be told to do by your DIs for the next three months will be considered a lawful order no matter how outrageous the command may seem.

Last, Article 89 will prohibit disrespect of a superior *commissioned* officer. Failure to salute an officer, for example, can constitute a violation of Article 89.

While on the yellow footprints, you'll be advised by a Receiving Drill Instructor that you're now *aboard* a United States Marine Corps Recruit Depot and that you've taken the first step to becoming a member of the *"World's Finest Fighting Force."* The DI will inform you that tens of thousands of Marines have begun their service on the very footsteps upon which you stand, and that it'll be your responsibility to carry on that proud tradition. You'll find out that pronouns like *I, me,* or *my* will no longer be a part of your vocabulary, and that you'll use only third-person referrals such as *this recruit, that recruit,* and *these recruits.* You'll also quickly learn that speed, intensity, and volume when speaking are a must. An extremely important thing to remember is that you should never, ever say the word, "you" to a Drill Instructor. A "ewe", which is phonetically identical to the word "you," is a female sheep, and Drill Instructors take it very personally when you call them a female sheep.

Once you right-face off of the footprints, you'll be ushered toward the *Receiving Barracks,* which is the barracks in which you'll spend the remainder of Receiving Week. Upon this barracks and above its front door, or *portal* as it's called in the Marine Corps, is the famous statement, *"Through These Portals Pass Prospects for America's Finest Fighting Force."* Once you pass through these portals, no matter what kind of wild ideas you may come up with to back out of your decision to become a Marine (such as faking your hearing test or curling up in the fetal position and sucking your thumb), you'll be better off resigning yourself to the fact that you're going to spend the next 13 weeks giving it your all. Drill Instructors have seen nearly every trick in the book, and the only experience more difficult than Marine Recruit Training is the plight of those who try to get out of Marine Recruit Training once they get there.

As you enter the Receiving Barracks, you'll be seated in school-like desks where you'll remain for hours upon end. You're in-processing will then begin. Make sure that you keep your mouth shut unless you're spoken to, and under no circumstances smile. Don't plan on getting any sleep for the first three days unless you can do it sitting up with your eyes open.

In Receiving, you'll be given the opportunity to call home and let your loved ones know that you've arrived safely. You'll be reading from a script, and won't be allowed to say any more than what's written on the paper, so don't make the mistake of trying to slip in a few extra words. My advice is to read the scripted message, then simply hang up. You'll get a chance to write home in a few days, and you can elaborate on anything you feel like saying then.

Knowing that I would need to focus solely on Recruit Training and not home, I wrote one letter explaining to my family that I wouldn't be writing them and asked them not to write me. While others spent their daily hour of free-time writing, I chose to clean my weapon, polish my boots, shine my brass, and study Marine Corps knowledge. If you want to do well in Recruit Training, I'd suggest you do the same. The Marine Corps frowns on putting anything before itself. For example, it's understood that if the Marine Corps wanted you to have a wife, they would *issue* you one.

As Receiving progresses, you'll be searched for contraband, and ordered to surrender all of your personal items including your underwear. You'll then receive an initial uniform issue, including underwear, as well as basic toiletries. You'll nod off in your desk because it's virtually impossible not to, and you'll get screamed at for doing it. Eventually, you'll be assigned to a bed in a Receiving *squad bay* where you'll lay down long enough to ask yourself, *"what in the hell am I doing here?"* You'll sleep a few hours, then it'll start all over again the next morning.

Over the course of the remainder of the week, you'll get to catch a little more sleep (very little), sign lots and lots of paperwork, and get your head shaved if you're a male or cut extremely short if you're a *WM,* or *Woman Marine.* You'll also undergo a great deal of medical and dental screening including a drug screen, and receive numerous vaccinations. In time, you'll receive your service rifle with orders to keep it within arm's reach at all times. This is no joke. Losing your M16 can be a court-martial offense.

At some point during receiving, your temporary Drill Instructors will appoint from your platoon a temporary *Guide* and four *Squad Leaders* to assist them with the platoon through delegation of authority. The platoon Guide position will be the highest recruit leadership position available, and he or she will be appointed by your Senior Drill Instructor. Among many other duties, the Guide will be responsible for carrying the platoon *guidon,* or flag. The Guide will report directly to the Senior Drill Instructor, but will take orders from all Drill Instructors.

A Squad Leader is also a leadership position. There are four Squad Leaders per platoon, each responsible for the recruits of his or her squad. Squad Leaders report directly to the platoon Guide. The Senior

Drill Instructor can (and will) hire and fire Guides and Squad Leaders throughout the course of Recruit Training as he or she sees fit.

Keep in mind that, near the end of Receiving, you'll be given your IST to ensure that you're good-to-go physically. The IST is a scaled-down version of the PFT, and consists of a timed mile-and-a-half run, pull-ups, and a two-minute crunch session. If you haven't been training, this is where it'll show. If you show up way out of shape or way overweight and fail the IST, you'll more than likely be pulled out of training and placed into *PCP* or the *Physical Conditioning Platoon* until your IST score improves. Once you can pass the test, you'll fall back into training. Unfortunately, you'll fall back in with a company whose schedule runs behind the one you arrived with. How far back you fall in depends on how many weeks you spend in PCP.

On Friday of Receiving Week, you'll be *picked up* by your permanent Company, moved to your permanent barracks, and introduced to your permanent Drill Instructors. This day is ominously known as *Black Friday,* and will become a day that you'll never forget.

Chapter 3: Black Friday

AVERAGE AMERICANS KNOW *Black Friday* as the busiest shopping day of the year. Marines know it for its real meaning. Black Friday is the day that your Marine Corps Recruit Training will officially begin. It's the day you'll be picked up by your permanent Drill Instructors and transferred to your permanent barracks and squad bay. It's also the day that you'll learn to which specific battalion, company, platoon, squad, and fire team you'll been assigned.

The first couple of days with your permanent Drill Instructors are known as *Forming*. After about 72 hours of Forming, your full-blown training will begin. From Training Day 1 (T1) forward, you'll begin a three-phase program that can transform you from a recruit into a bona fide United State Marine. Phase 1 (T1-T23) will last about four weeks with heavy emphasis placed upon physical conditioning and breaking you of your civilian mindset. Phase 2 (T24-T47) will last approximately four weeks and will focus on marksmanship training. Phase 3 (T48-T70) will last about four weeks and will concentrate mainly on field training. All of this very intense training will take place under the watchful eye of your Drill Instructors, who you'll initially want to hate, but eventually hold in the highest esteem.

Generally speaking, the duty of a Drill Instructor is to supervise and instruct a Marine recruit platoon. Just like in the movies, Marine Corps Drill Instructors are the stuff of legends. After your recruiter, they're your first impression of the Marine Corps, so naturally they've been carefully selected from the ranks to provide you with the knowledge and training that you'll need to become a Marine. Without question, Marine Drill Instructors are the "cream of the crop" as far as Marines go, and it'll behoove you to emulate them as role models.

More specifically, your Drill Instructors will conduct your Recruit Training while strictly adhering to a pre-determined *training schedule* and *orders*, both of which come down from the *Commandant of the*

Marine Corps (CMC), the highest ranking officer in the Corps. Your DIs will instruct you and assist you in basic combat tasks, and train you in the fundamentals of service life and the development of discipline, physical fitness, pride, and love of the Marine Corps and country. You'll be taught by your Drill Instructors how to perform close-order drill, and they'll familiarize you in the nomenclature, disassembly, assembly, and functioning of various small arms. This will include assistance in marksmanship instruction.

Other examples of the duties of Drill Instructors are instruction in General Orders, interior guard duty, personal hygiene, first aid, military bearing and neatness, and care of clothing and equipment. Your DIs will also lecture you on Marine Corps history and tradition, customs of service, military courtesy, and U.S. Naval Regulations. During Recruit Training your Drill Instructors, who are masters of multitasking, will even maintain records and prepare reports while performing all of these other duties. Most notably, Drill Instructors will sacrifice the comforts of their homes and time with their families in order to remain with you throughout your training process.

Once you arrive at your permanent barracks, you'll be seated "Indian style" in columns and rows on the *Quarterdeck.* There you'll meet your Company Commander and Chief Drill Instructor. After a brief orientation about their roles in your training, you'll be introduced by them to your Senior Drill Instructor. Your Senior DI is the "good cop" in the proverbial "good cop-bad cop" routine. Senior Drill Instructors are distinguished by a black sword belt (or Sam Browne Belt, but without the shoulder strap). The Senior will be ultimately responsible for the training of your platoon. Your Senior Drill Instructor will also be accountable for the effectiveness of his or her Assistant Drill Instructors.

The "bad cops" are the Assistant or Junior Drill Instructors, and are identified by their green webbed duty belts. Typically, a platoon will have one Senior and three Junior Drill Instructors. Second in command to the Senior is called the *Second Hat,* or *Heavy,* and will be primarily responsible for teaching close-order drill. The junior-most DIs are often called *Kill Hats* because of their propensity to dole out punishment to deserving recruits. Junior Drill Instructors are assigned to Recruit Training Battalions to, among other duties, administer constant corrections by way of dispensing punitive *Incentive Training,* or *IT.*

Essentially, Incentive Training consists of physical exercises that are administered by Drill Instructors in an extremely controlled and deliberate fashion. IT is a time-tested, battle proven tool that's used for the purpose of correcting minor disciplinary infractions and to instill strength, discipline and motivation in recruits. Some of the exercises used in IT are side-straddle hops (jumping jacks), bends-and-thrusts, mountain climbers, and running in place. Incentive Training will begin for you on day one of Forming and will continue through day 68. As soon as you're instructed on IT, Drill Instructors will be free to utilize it, and you can rest assured that they will.

While in your squad bay, which is the bunking area inside of the barracks, you'll often be IT'd on the quarterdeck. This is also known as *quarterdecking.* On a ship, the quarterdeck is reserved for ship's officers, guests, and passengers. In keeping with that naval tradition, Drill Instructors maintain the barracks quarterdeck as their own. Located near the instructor's office, or *house,* the quarterdeck will be off-limits to you and other recruits except during periods of discipline. When you err (and you will), you'll be called to the quarterdeck by a Drill Instructor, where you'll undergo constant, repetitive physical exercise until your Drill Instructor is satisfied with your punishment. When your entire platoon needs to be IT'd, it'll often take place outside of the barracks in a sand filled area known as the *pit,* or the *beach.* While at Recruit Training, you and the rest of your platoon will spend an awful lot of time at the beach.

In an attempt to create exceptional leaders starting at the recruit level, Guides and Squad Leaders will be IT'd for the shortcomings and mistakes of the entire platoon. During my time at Recruit Training, I paid for virtually every mistake made by every recruit in my platoon. I spent so much time on the Quarterdeck, in the pit, and on the ground somewhere, that I eventually got into such good shape that the Drill Instructors would actually get bored trying to wear me out, and would move on to something or someone else.

As with other Recruit Training challenges, I believe that I responded well to IT because of the mindset that I possessed. The precept that many recruits fail to comprehend, is that even though IT is perceived as punishment by the Drill Instructors, it is, in its essence, physical conditioning—and physical conditioning is a good thing, especially when training for survival in a combat environment. Therefore, Incentive Training, like many other things, was a matter of perception for me. I chose to perceive it as a positive. To me, after paying hundreds maybe thousands of dollars in gym dues, I simply looked at IT as if I was getting paid to work out. The point is, your mindset can "make you or break you."

Something worth noting though, is that once your platoon starts experiencing IT sessions, you'll discover that there will be basically two types of recruits on board: One type will be a conservative, patriotic-minded recruit who sees his enlistment as a duty owed his nation. The other will be a liberal, "entitlement" recruit who views his or her enlistment as a means for personal gain such as glory or solely as a way to receive a free education. In a battlefield environment, the former will most always lay down his life for his fellow Marines, while the latter will oftentimes declare himself or herself a *conscientious objector* and refuse to fight. The conservative recruit knows that IT has been a successful means of ensuring that the Marine Corps has remained the *"World's Finest Fighting Force"* for over two centuries, and gladly welcomes it as part of his or her "rite of passage." The entitlement recruit, on the other hand, will more than likely reject the concept of IT once he or she is subjected to it for any length of time.

Once the notion of IT has been rejected by the entitlement recruit, he or she will then usually reach out to his liberal-minded mother or father via a letter, and allege Drill Instructor "abuse." In turn, the liberal parents, rather than telling their child to "suck it up" as other Marine parents have done for decades, will often choose to contact their liberal legislators, convey the alleged abuse, and pressure those legislators to provide their child relief by way of the political system.

Sadly, due to past *legitimate* abuses by overzealous Drill Instructors, "safeguards" have been put in place to limit the amount of IT to which a recruit may be subjected. Although this act can grant temporary relief to the entitlement recruits who want to be *gifted* the title of Marine, the net effect of this scheme is a lesser trained Marine in the battlefield, which weakens the Corps as a whole. Because IT is the primary means of instilling within recruits the strength, discipline and motivation necessary to master combat survival skills, to "kneecap" a judicious Drill Instructor's ability to subject a recruit to IT as he or she sees fit will obviously increase battlefield casualties and ultimately weaken our national defense.

Oftentimes your Drill Instructors will use IT to "weed out" those recruits whom they perceive as detrimental to the Corps. As a patriot who desires to serve the United States, you have a duty to support the efforts of those judicious Drill Instructors who attempt to get rid of those recruits who wish to usurp the requirements necessary to *earn* the title. Remember, the liberal legislators won't be on the battlefield with you—history shows that they'll be too busy doing everything within their legislative power to undermine the United States, its *Constitution,* and our military. Neither will it be those liberal-minded parents who attempt to legislate Marine Corps policy from the comfort of their homes—they'll be too busy trying to figure out what our country can do for them at the expense of the blood, sweat, and tears of patriotic Americans like you and others who so selflessly volunteer to defend freedom. It'll be *you* on the battlefield, alongside your fellow Marines. By supporting your Drill

Instructors' efforts to weed out those who essentially attempt to *steal* the title Marine rather than earn it, you'll have an active voice in who those fellow Marines will be.

Some good news is that Drill Instructors are not always as daunting as they appear. At times they can even be quite comical. In my platoon, we had a recruit whose last name was *Queer*. The first time this was revealed to one of our Junior Drill Instructors, the DI was absolutely ecstatic and spent about 15 minutes questioning Queer about his name.

The Drill Instructor, standing nose-to-nose with Recruit Queer and doing everything he could to restrain a smile, bellowed, *"You mean to tell me you're doggone name is Queer? That means you're a faggot, right?"*

"Sir no sir!" Queer said.

"Then what's your stinkin' name son?"

"Sir, Queer sir."

"Then that means you're a queer doesn't it?"

"Sir no sir!

"Then what was your father's last name recruit?

"Sir, Queer sir!

"Oh yeah? And you're mother's last name was Queer?

"Sir yes sir."

"If they were Queers then that means you're a queer, right?"

"Sir, I guess so sir."

"What do you mean, you guess so? Your last name's Queer, right?"

"Sir yes sir."

"Then you're a queer!"

"Sir yes sir."

"Hahaha, I knew it! Then that means you must suck dick!"

"Sir no sir."

"Go away Queer. You're not foolin' anyone."

From that day forward, every time our platoon met another, the DI would stop our training, summon the staff from the other platoon and, with an ostensibly serious expression disguising his smile say, *"Ask him what his name is."* Most of the time, the staff would walk away shaking their heads while envisioning what a tough row the recruit would have to hoe. Other staff would engage Queer in a question and answer session similar to our Drill Instructor's. Each time this happened, Queer grew tougher. By the time we graduated, Recruit Queer had become one of the most outstanding Marines of our platoon.

Recruit Queer could have made a conscious decision to write home to his family and complain about the seemingly prejudicial treatment. He could've even filed a complaint with the DI's superiors and the superiors probably would've intervened. However, Queer knew that Drill Instructors are Drill Instructors for a reason, and that the reason is to ensure Marines are victorious in combat—*period.*

To better understand what I believe was the purpose of the interaction between Recruit Queer and the Drill Instructor, I would suggest that you listen to the words of the Johnny Cash song, *"A Boy Named Sue."* In the song, a boy who has been named "Sue" by his father is so bitter from having to fight all of his life because of his name, that when he grows up, he hunts his father down with the intention of killing him. Once the son locates the father, and after the son bests him in a fist-fight, the father, who cares deeply for his son, explains to the son why he named him Sue. The father says,

"This world is rough and if a man's gonna make it, he's gotta be tough and I knew I wouldn't be there to help you along. So I give you that name and I said goodbye, I knew you'd have to get tough or die and it's that name that helped to make you strong."

Like the father in the song who cared for his son's future yet who knew that he wouldn't always be around, the Drill Instructor also cared about the future of Recruit Queer, and knew that he wouldn't always be around to watch over Queer during dangerous times, specifically in times of war. Consequently, the Drill Instructor did what he judged best in order to mold Queer into the toughest Marine possible, all the while knowing that if Queer whined and claimed that he was "offended" or that he was being "abused," then that would be a clue that the recruit wasn't tough enough— or wise enough— to become a Marine anyway.

As Black Friday comes to a close, you'll have a pretty good idea of what your daily routine will be like for the rest of Recruit Training. Although days will vary, a typical day will begin before sunrise with the lights coming on while every recruit in your barracks simultaneously screams, "LIGHTS!" Once up, you'll present yourself *on line* at the foot of your rack for count. When all recruits are accounted for, you'll be allowed a few minutes for personal hygiene, then your platoon will perform *morning clean-up.*

After all bunks are correctly made and your barracks is squared away, your platoon will form up outside and perform physical training (PT). PT will almost always entail the *Marine Corps Daily Dozen,* a set of calisthenics designed to help you maintain full body health and fitness. Once PT is completed, you'll then form up and march to the chow hall for morning chow. After slamming a moderate amount of food at a high rate of speed, you'll begin the day's scheduled training.

After noon chow, you'll continue your training until your evening meal, which will typically be served around 1800. After evening chow, you'll have a few minutes to shower, clean your weapon, and square away your barracks. As each day comes to an end, you'll be allowed an hour of personal time before lights out, which usually occurs around 2200. It'll be very important for you to sleep as quickly and as much as possible once lights are out, because when Phase 1 begins, sleep will be one of the scarcest resources available. On Sundays, you'll have an opportunity to attend church, and you'll be allowed a short period of personal time to *square away* your gear.

Chapter 4: Phase 1

PHASE 1 WILL last approximately four weeks. Simply put, the primary objective of Phase 1 will be to break you down psychologically through confusion and disorientation, with the end goal of diminishing your civilian mindset and creating within you the mindset of a Marine. This will be done through intense physical training, consistent "by-the-numbers" routines, strict discipline, and voluminous periods of instruction. The purpose of this mindset change will be to enable you to better comprehend what's to come during the remainder of Recruit Training, and ultimately, enable you to survive in combat.

The majority of Phase 1 instruction will consist of classes on Marine Corps history, first aid, rank structure, rank insignia, protocol, customs and courtesies, uniform regulations, and other relevant topics. You'll learn most of this information through what's known as *rote learning* and *mnemonics*. Rote learning is the memorization of information through repetition. An example of rote learning would be the way you learned to recite the alphabet in grammar school. A mnemonic is a device such as a pattern of letters, ideas, or associations that assists in recalling information from your memory. An example of a mnemonic would be an *acronym,* such as "NATO," which stands for "North Atlantic Treaty Organization."

During your first week of Phase 1 training, you'll learn a completely new language of Marine Corps terminology, all of which has been founded on naval tradition. A floor will become a *deck,* and a wall will become a *bulkhead.* Front will become *forward,* or *fore,* and rear will become *aft.* A window will become a *porthole,* and a door will become a *hatch* or *portal.* Initially you'll become somewhat confused, but in time, you'll begin to see that there's a "method to the madness" of Recruit Training. Once you realize this, you'll start to form a feeling of contempt for the chaos and disorder of inferior civilian life. As the feeling of contempt grows, you'll become aware of the self-evident truth that if everyone was a

Marine, the world would be a much better and much safer place.

During the beginning of your training, the importance of the terms, *Honor, Courage, and Commitment* will be emphasized. These three words make up the "Core Values" of a Marine. These values define how every Marine should think, act, and fight.

Core Values

1. **Honor**: This is the bedrock of a Marine's character. It is the quality that empowers Marines to exemplify the ultimate in ethical and moral behavior: to never lie, cheat, or steal; to abide by an uncompromising code of integrity; to respect human dignity; and to have respect and concern for each other. It represents the maturity, dedication, trust, and dependability that commit Marines to act responsibly, be accountable for their actions, fulfill their obligations, and hold

others accountable for their actions.

2. **Courage:** The heart of a Marine's Core Values, courage is the mental, moral, and physical strength ingrained in Marines that sees them through the challenges of combat and the mastery of fear, and to do what is right, to adhere to a higher standard of personal conduct, to lead by example, and to make tough decisions under stress and pressure. It's the inner strength that enables a Marine to take that extra step.

3. **Commitment:** This is the spirit of determination and dedication within the Marine Corps that leads to professionalism and mastery of the art of war. It promotes the highest order of discipline for the unit and self, and is the ingredient that instills 24-hour per day dedication to Corps and Country, pride, concern for others, and an unrelenting determination to achieve a standard of excellence in every endeavor. Commitment is the value that establishes the Marine

as the warrior and citizen others strive to emulate.

When studying Core Values, it's vital that you understand that the Values are only abstract ideas which have no physical or concrete existence. You can read them all day every day, and even memorize them, but until you apply them, they are still no more to you than concepts, or words on paper. It's only when you personify these values, or represent them in human form, that they become tangible and real to you.

To assist you in developing the mindset of a Marine *before* you arrive at MCRD, try applying these values to your everyday life among family, friends, and co-workers. If you apply them over and over, your actions will soon become habitual, or habits. Ultimately, the more you do this, the more those habits will begin to reflect on your character, and eventually transform your character into one that embodies the Core Values of a United States Marine. It's sort of like the belief that if you smile enough, you'll eventually become happy.

Another example of Phase 1 knowledge is the military Code of Conduct, which was established to prepare U.S. troops for possible enemy captivity. Although you won't be required to memorize the Code, nor will you be tested on its origins, you'll certainly want to understand and be able to convey the precept behind the Code.

Code of Conduct

I. I am an American, fighting in the forces which guard my country and our way of life. I am prepared to give my life in their defense.

II. I will never forget that I am an American, fighting for freedom, responsible for my actions, and dedicated to the principles which made my country free. I will trust in my God and in the United States of America.

III. I will never surrender of my own free will. If in command, I will never surrender the members of my command while they still have the means to resist.

IV. If I am captured I will continue to resist by all means available. I will make every effort to escape and aid others to escape. I will accept neither parole nor special favors from the enemy.

V. If I become a prisoner of war, I will keep faith with my fellow prisoners. I will give no information or take part in any action which might be harmful to my comrades. If I am senior, I will take command. If not, I will obey the lawful orders of those appointed over me and will back them up in every way.

VI. When questioned, should I become a prisoner of war, I am required to give name, rank, service number, and date of birth. I will evade answering further questions to the utmost of my ability. I will make no oral or written statements disloyal to my country and its allies or harmful to their cause.

Something you *will* want to memorize are The 11 General Orders of a Sentry. I couldn't begin to count how many times I had to recite one or more of these orders while at MCRD. Recruits and Marines alike will be expected to know and recite (word for word) the 11 General Orders when standing guard duty or watch.

The 11 General Order of a Sentry

1. To take charge of this post and all government property in view.
2. To walk my post in a military manner, keeping always on the alert and observing everything that takes place within sight or hearing.
3. To report all violations of orders I am instructed to enforce.
4. To repeat all calls [from posts] more distant from the guardhouse than my own.
5. To quit my post only when properly relieved.
6. To receive, obey, and pass on to the sentry who relieves me, all orders from the Commanding Officer, Officer of the Day, Officers, and Non-Commissioned Officers of the guard only.
7. To talk to no one except in the line of duty.
8. To give the alarm in case of fire or disorder.

9. To call the Corporal of the Guard in any case not covered by instructions.
10. To salute all officers, colors, and standards not cased.
11. To be especially watchful at night, and during the time for challenging, to challenge all persons on or near my post and to allow no one to pass without proper authority.

Additionally, Phase 1 will require you to start compounding upon the close-order drill techniques that began when you formed up on the yellow footprints of Receiving. During close-order drill, constant repetition and practice will be used to instill muscle memory, so that any given movement can be performed immediately and precisely when you're ordered to do so. To aid in close-order drill, movements will be integrated into other parts of your everyday Recruit Training life. For example, when in the *chow hall,* you'll have to hold your tray with your arms in a position similar to the way you'll hold your rifle during "shoulder arms."

During Phase 1 you'll have an opportunity to work toward your Tan Belt in the *Marine Corps Martial Arts Program (MCMAP)*. This program will train you in unarmed combat, edged weapons, weapons of opportunity, and rifle and bayonet techniques. MCMAP draws influences from several martial arts disciplines including Brazilian Jiu-Jitsu, Greco-Roman Wrestling, Boxing, Savate, Jujutsu, Judo, Sambo, Krav Maga, Isshin Ryu, Karate, Aikido, Muay Thai, Eskrima, Hapkido, Taekwondo, Kung Fu, and Kickboxing. MCMAP also incorporates *warrior ethos training* which focuses on past history's warriors such as the Spartans, the Zulu, the Apache, as well as the Marine Raiders of World War II.

Tan Belt training is the minimum basic requirement for all Marines, and will include an introduction to the fundamentals of the mental, character, and physical disciplines of MCMAP. Warfighting concepts, character values, and the basic fighting techniques required of a basically trained Marine will also be included in your Tan Belt training. Becoming an *ethical warrior* ensures that you'll not only be trained in "fighting," but that you'll also possess the mental discipline necessary to develop an ethical warrior's mindset.

To earn your tan belt, you'll have to prove proficient with 70% of 50 different techniques. You'll begin with the Basic Warrior Stance, then progress to:

- Basic punches, uppercuts, and hooks;
- Basic upper-body strikes, including the eye gouge, hammer fists, and elbow strikes;
- Basic lower-body strikes, including kicks, knee strikes, and stomps;
- Bayonet techniques;
- Basic chokes, joint locks, and throws;
- Counters to strikes, chokes, and holds;
- Basic unarmed restraints and armed manipulations;
- Basic knife techniques;
- Basic weapons of opportunity.

During your time in the Marine Corps, you'll be able to advance through five different colored belt levels:

- Tan Belt
- Gray Belt
- Green Belt
- Brown Belt
- Black Belt (1st degree through 6th degree)

If you're able to make it to the third week of Phase 1, you'll have an opportunity to experience the Marine Corps *Confidence Course* which, as its name implies, is designed to build your self-confidence. The Marine Corps Confidence Course is made up of several obstacles, each progressively more difficult than the one before it. All recruits will have an opportunity to negotiate the Confidence Course several times during Recruit Training. Each time my platoon ran the Confidence Course, it was a major game changer for those who had previously underestimated their abilities. Many recruits who were initially intimidated by the course walked away from it highly motivated once they completed it, and looked forward to challenging it again.

Week three of first phase will also require you to stand a *Senior Drill Instructor's Inspection.* Inspections will be an integral part of your life in the Marine Corps and will reinforce the importance of combat readiness. The Senior Drill Instructor Inspection will be the first of three major inspections that you'll undergo during Recruit Training. During this inspection, you'll be graded on personal appearance, hygiene, weapon cleanliness, and Marine Corps knowledge.

Week four of Phase 1 is known as *Swim Week.* Once you reach week four, you'll face your first graduation requirement—*Swim Qualification.* The reason for this requirement is because, by definition, Marines are an *amphibious fighting force.* Consequently, Marines must be amphibious by nature and must know how to survive in the water. In order to give you a basic understanding of water survival, the Marine Corps has developed what is known as *Marine Corps Combat Water Survival Training.* During this training, which will take place in an indoor pool environment, you'll learn to leap into deep water, to tread water, to use your issued equipment to stay afloat, and to shed heavy gear that could pull you underwater.

Swim Week will be where your platoon will lose several recruits who aren't as proficient at swimming as they should be. These recruits will be known as *swim uncs,* short for *swim unqualifieds.* Swim uncs will be *dropped* from your platoon and *recycled* to a following company until their swimming skills improve.

Keep in mind that Swim Week won't be as much about swimming as it will be about being able to confidently survive while treading water. The intent of the *Combat Water Survival Training Program* is to reduce fear of water, raise self-confidence, and develop your ability to survive in aquatic environments. In layman's (or laywoman's) terms, this means that you really just need to know how to dogpaddle and not be scared while doing it. Still, many recruits will fail to qualify.

Once you're ready to begin qualification, you'll start the course with a 25-meter swim in shallow water. Immediately afterward, you'll jump from a 15-foot platform into the deep end of the pool, where you'll emerge, swim to a nearby area, and tread water for four minutes. Once four minutes have elapsed, you'll then swim another 25 meters. *That's it.* And you'll do this with no gear on—just your basic utility uniform. Once you've completed the initial swim event, you'll have met the Marine Corps' current *minimum* swim qualification graduation requirement, and will be able to move on to Phase 2.

For those of you who want to achieve a superior level of water survival skill, two more classes of qualifications are available—both of these classes involving full combat gear. If you decide to attempt the next level, you'll begin by entering the water and swimming 25 meters. You'll then don full combat gear, enter shallow water, and swim 40 meters to the other side of the pool.

Once you've reached the other side, you'll climb onto an eight-foot platform, then jump back into the pool. When you've recovered from your jump by surfacing, you'll then swim 25 meters to completion.

The final level that you'll be able to obtain while at Recruit Training focuses on assisting an immobile recruit to safety while wearing full combat gear. Beginning with a 50-meter swim, you'll latch onto and drag another recruit 25 meters to safety. This, of course, will simulate an actual water rescue.

Whether or not you'll attempt to qualify at the minimum level or higher will be up to you. Personally, I feel that you should approach the swim qual just like you would the PFT. That is to say, I would aim for the highest level of swim qualification, and you'll find that you'll excel during Swim Week. As a Marine, you'll oftentimes find yourself in aquatic environments, and when you do, you'll want to enter those environments with the utmost confidence in you swimming ability—especially if you find yourself conducting an open-water rescue of a fellow Marine. Additionally, if you aspire to become a *Special Operator,* such as a *Force Recon* Marine, then you'll want to be able to negotiate the water as proficiently as possible.

As Phase 1 comes to an end, you'll start to sense the transformation that's taking place in the way you look, act, think, and believe. Once you've completed Phase 1, you'll look like, act like, think like, and believe like a Marine *recruit* rather than a civilian. Being a recruit however, is a far cry from being a Marine. Transitioning from Phase 1 to Phase 2 will allow you to begin building upon your newfound skills, and move you one step closer to becoming a full-fledged United States Marine.

Chapter 5: Phase 2

UNTIL THE BEGINNING of Phase 2, when the Guide will be allowed to place a flag, or *colors,* on his guidon, your platoon has had to bear the guidon with no colors attached. The significance of the absence of colors is to show others that a platoon is in its infancy, untrained, and unorganized. To understand the significance of Phase 2, it's important that you understand the significance of the platoon guidon.

Since ancient times, the guidon has been a great source of pride for military units. The guidon represents a unit and the unit's commander, and is a rallying point for troops to fall into formation when the *"Fall in"* order is given. Combat-wise, unit colors have been a source of pride, in that victories or defeats in battle often culminated with the capture of the enemy's colors.

Likewise, it's also a tremendous source of pride to be the guidon bearer because it affords the bearer an opportunity to stand in front of the unit alongside the unit's commander (or the commander's representative). However, with the advancement of modern warfare, it's no longer prudent to point out the location of the commander with a guidon—there have been far too many commanders targeted and killed as a result. Nevertheless, the guidon is still used extensively at MCRD to identify platoons and to build the platoon's *esprit de corps.*

It's also important for you to understand that over time, military traditions have evolved around the guidon. For instance, to disgrace a guidon is to disgrace the entire unit, and is likened to disgracing one's mother—an act that most always demands retribution. Additionally, during Recruit Training, members of other platoons will try to steal another platoon's guidon, and vice versa. I was successfully able to do this, which was an incredible morale-booster for my platoon. On the same token, it was a tremendous blow to the platoon—and its guide—from whom the guidon was "captured," and they were harshly punished for their loss.

At times, Drill Instructors will try to snatch the guidon from an opposing platoon's Guide, and some will even *order* an opposing Guide to relinquish it to them. This tactic always creates a precarious situation for its bearer when considering Article 91 of the UCMJ. Usually though, when something like this happens, one of your own Drill Instructors will come to the rescue.

Should you end up the Guide, and should a superior officer from another platoon attempt to order you to relinquish your guidon, I would highly recommend that you disobey that order. This is one instance when you'll be rewarded rather than punished for your disobedience. If you think you might be a Guide, then it's paramount that you understand the significance of relinquishing the guidon, and that an attempt to get you to do so is nothing more than a test to see how committed you are to your platoon and to the Corps. In real-world terms, to give up the guidon is no different than giving up your entire platoon to the enemy. It's considered an act of treason.

On Training Day 24, which is the first day of Phase 2, the Guide will have the privilege of attaching the Phase 2 colors onto the guidon. The Phase 2 colors are gold with scarlet numbers signifying the platoon's number. Flying the Phase 2 colors was another incredible morale-booster for myself and the rest of the platoon. Doing so allowed us to feel like we were real Marines. During the preceding weeks, we had been paraded around Parris Island by our drill instructors with our naked guidon pole, looking like an inebriated troupe of circus clowns. For the better part of Phase 1, most Recruits didn't know a rifle barrel from a rifle butt. In our minds, once we were allowed to fly the Phase 2 colors, we were somehow instantly transformed into hardened Marines. Becoming Marines, of course, was yet to come.

Phase 2 will last approximately four weeks. It will begin with the *Initial Drill Evaluation,* where the Company's platoons *and* the platoons' junior-most Drill Instructors will each be graded as a whole on their performance of close-order drill. In addition to overall drill performance, the platoons will also be graded on personal hygiene, uniform neatness, and the cleanliness of their weapons. Initial Drill will give each platoon a chance to see how well they can instantly follow orders as a unit rather than as individuals, and will play a vital role in the development of unit solidarity.

As Phase 2 continues, you'll have your yearbook photos taken, get haircuts (again), and pay a visit to clothing, where you'll be measured for your permanent uniforms. Some of you will visit dental, and all of you will perform lots of IT. Every recruit will also be required to take the *Initial Written Test,* undergo *rappelling* training, and *experience the gas chamber.*

Prior to visiting the gas chamber, you'll be given a period of instruction on the use of your gas mask. Pay close attention to instruction on how to *don and clear* your mask. Not only will you need to pay attention because of your training requirements, but also because your gas mask can mean the difference between life and death on the battlefield. Many *jihadist,* or Muslims who advocate the spread of the religion *Islam* by way of violence, have vowed to develop and use *NBC* (Nuclear, Biological, and Chemical) weaponry against the United States and its allies.

Once you enter the gas chamber, you'll be required to perform various exercises with and without your mask on. Each of you will experience the effects of *CS* gas on your eyes, nose, and skin. Some recruits will panic and attempt to run out of the door during the exercise. A little-known tradition among Drill Instructors is to open-field tackle those fleeing recruits as they run out of the gas chamber door. Whether those who attempt to flee are tackled or not, they'll be ordered to return into the chamber. If they refuse, they'll be immediately dropped from the platoon and recycled.

Rappelling will also be a highlight of Phase 2. Rappelling is a controlled descent from a great height using a harness and ropes as a pulley system. Rappelling will prepare you for deployment from helicopters, for descending down difficult terrain, and for assaulting structures during an urban attack. Oftentimes helicopter landings are impractical, therefore Marines must possess the ability to conduct insertions and extractions from a hovering chopper, or *bird*. Likewise, Marines must know how to descend into mountainous ravines, such as those that exist along the Afghanistan-Pakistan border, a known haven for terrorists. Just as well, modernization and increased urban warfare demand that a Marine know how to breach enemy-held buildings by way of rappelling, such as entering a window after inserting by helicopter onto a roof.

Week two of Phase 2 is known as *Grass Week,* and is an introduction to the *Marine Corps Combat Marksmanship Program.* Because a Marine's rifle is the primary means by which he or she obtains dominance over the enemy and neutralizes the effects of enemy weapons, a Marine must be able to competently and effectively employ the service rifle under virtually any condition. Marine Corps *Primary Marksmanship Instructors,* or *PMIs,* are experts at ensuring that you'll be able to do this.

A good portion of Grass Week will be spent in a classroom environment sitting through periods of instruction on how to fire your weapon. You'll learn the acronym, *BRASS-F,* which stands for *Breath, Relax, Aim, Squeeze, Shoot, Follow-through*, and learn to apply these steps to perfect your shooting. When not in the classroom, you'll be at the firing range *snapping in,* or practicing the four firing positions: *prone*, *sitting, standing*, and *kneeling*. At the range, PMIs will spend plenty of time with you teaching you how to adjust your sights in relation to distance and environmental conditions such as wind. Even though PMIs look and dress like Drill Instructors, they aren't DIs, so they won't act like them. Because of the importance of marksmanship training, PMIs will be focused solely on teaching you how to become a world-class rifle expert. During Grass Week, I found that even my Drill Instructors loosened up while at the range, often sharing with me their tips on becoming a better marksman.

The third week of Phase 2 is known as *Firing Week.* This is the week where you'll come to realize that you've chosen a pretty serious occupation. During Firing Week, you'll be awakened earlier than usual in order to prepare the rifle range for firing. You'll spend all day firing live rounds on the *Known Distance Course,* or *KD Course.* Half of the platoons will fire at the 200, 300, and 500 yard lines, and the other half will *pull butts.* Pulling butts means working in the target pits behind a berm and below the targets. Then the platoons will switch, giving everyone an opportunity to either work the range, or fire on it.

Friday of Firing Week is the day that you'll put all of your marksmanship training to the test. This day is known as *Qual Day,* short for *Qualification Day.* On Qual Day, you must qualify with a minimum score in order to earn a marksmanship badge and continue with Recruit Training. Those who fail to qualify will be given one more chance during the following week, but if they fail again, they'll be dropped and will have to start over at Grass Week.

Once Qual Day is over, you'll do a 12km conditioning march on Saturday, then on Monday, you'll begin what is known as *Team Week.* Team Week is a week-long event that will afford you and the recruits of your Company an opportunity to work at various locations around MCRD alongside Marines and civilian workers. Throughout Team Week, you'll have an opportunity to interact with real-world Marines, and you'll be expected to carry yourself like one.

During Team Week, recruits, some of whom will be placed in leadership roles, will be required to put aside their differences in order to accomplish common goals. Although it'll be a much-needed break from your Drill Instructors and intensive training, like all things Marine, Team Week has definite objectives. A primary objective is to ensure that recruits learn to interact with each other more, which builds teamwork and camaraderie—vital attributes for successfully completing the upcoming 54-hour *Crucible*. Another purpose is to facilitate confident, effective communication between yourself and other Marines—a skill that you'll need once you graduate and reach a duty station.

During Team Week, you'll also have an opportunity to undergo necessary (or in my case, unnecessary) dental surgeries. Without any prior notice, I was called into Dental, where the dentist surgically removed four wisdom teeth, handed me a bottle of Motrin®, and sent me back to training. Although I can only speculate, I feel that this was an acceptable tactic used by the Marine Corps at the time to inflict as much stress as possible on a recruit in order to weed out the weak. My wisdom teeth were just fine. I'll probably never know the real reason, but I do know that it was quite a shocker. You know what they say though, *"what doesn't kill you makes you stronger."* In my case, that's exactly what it did—it made me stronger. I didn't care. They could've surgically removed a leg and it wouldn't have stopped me. My desire to become a Marine, combined with the mindset that I possessed from proper preparation, carried me on to Phase 3, and ultimately, on to graduation.

Team Week will culminate on Saturday with a *Company Commander's Inspection.* Similar to the Phase 1 Senior Drill Instructor's Inspection, this inspection will give your Company Commander an opportunity to test his or her recruits on their knowledge, while simultaneously reviewing their uniforms, military bearing, confidence, and weapons maintenance. The Commander will also use this time to ensure each recruit has met all the basic requirements to date in order to graduate Recruit Training.

The next morning you'll leave your barracks and travel to the *Weapons and Field Training Battalion,* or *WFTBn* for *BWT (Basic Warrior Training)* and *Table 2 Firing* week. There, you'll pair up with another recruit and each of you will attach your issued *shelter halves* together to form one two-man tent, or *hooch.* Once your platoon has successfully *bivouacked,* or set up camp, you'll form up with the rest of your platoon and begin preparatory classes for what will possibly be the most rigorous, but most rewarding, four weeks of your life—Phase 3 of Marine Corps Recruit Training.

Chapter 6: Phase 3

IF YOU'VE NEVER experienced Marine Recruit Training, then you'll probably never completely understand the feeling shared by a platoon when it first flies its Phase 3 guidon. To try to put it into words, if flying the Phase 2 guidon is euphoria, then flying the Phase 3 flag is bliss.

From the time Recruit Training began for me, every time our platoon was passed by a Third Phase platoon that was flying its scarlet flag with gold numbers, our DIs would say something like, *"Look at that platoon. Those are Third Phase Recruits. They could tear you apart."* Granted, statements like that from our Drill Instructors helped to create for us a certain mystique around the senior-most platoons. However, words weren't necessary for us to see that the Third Phase recruits were lethal. Their muscles bulged, their faces were tanned, and their heads and eyes remained fixed unflinchingly frontward. The soon-to-be Marines radiated an aura of maturity and discipline. With every step they took, each of their boot heals struck the ground simultaneously, emitting a noise like thunder. In unison, their lungs bellowed cadence as if it were the angel Gabriel sounding his trumpet. It was abundantly clear to us all that a Third Phase platoon was a force to be reckoned with—and we wanted to be like them.

Throughout Phase 3, your skills and knowledge will be refined, honed, and perfected, with the end goal of creating a more capable and less vulnerable combat-ready Marine. Although heavy emphasis will be placed on conventional battlefield techniques, you'll also be introduced to the concept of unconventional or *irregular warfare* through various periods of instruction such as *Terrorism Awareness, Combat Hunter,* and *Operational Culture.* In addition, Phase 3 will give you a chance to qualify for the *CFT,* or *Combat Fitness Test,* as well as an opportunity to run the Confidence Course again. As Phase 3 comes to an end, you'll take a *Final Written Exam,* run your *Final PFT,* and compete with the other platoons in *Final Drill.* You'll also attempt to complete the *Crucible.* If you're able to complete this grueling 54-hour challenge, you'll stand a *Battalion Commander's Inspection* and, on Training Day 70, graduate from Marine Recruit Training.

The first week of Phase 3 is known as *BWT/Table 2 Firing Week.* During *BWT,* you'll learn the basic fundamentals of combat while sleeping in the field and eating *MREs,* or *Meals Ready to Eat.* Some of the skills you'll be taught are the *art of camouflage, day and night land navigation, tactical formations, patrolling,* and other foundations of military skills. In a remote, unfamiliar environment, you'll also begin to hone your sense of *situational awareness.* Situational awareness is the degree of accuracy by which your perception of your current environment mirrors reality—a sensory perception that's vital when attempting to avoid *IEDs,* or *Improvised Explosive Devices,* and other potential combat dangers.

BWT will also incorporate Table 2 firing, where you'll learn to fire and have to qualify with your weapon under more realistic combat conditions like unknown distances, at night, and while wearing a gas mask. Table 2 firing will give you an opportunity to fire at moving targets from a *combat stance* rather than from a competition-style stance as you did during Firing Week.

An important irregular warfare course that you'll be introduced to during week one of Phase 3 is the *Combat Hunter* training program. Because the Marine Corps has a proud tradition of taking the fight to the enemy under complex and challenging conditions, it'll be important for you to develop and hone a tactical, cunning mindset in order to outsmart a thinking enemy. Combat Hunter was developed by the Marine Corps using world renowned big-game hunters, experienced police officers, expert trackers, Marine Infantry trainers, and human performance training and education experts provided by the *Office of Naval Research.* The Combat Hunter program will teach you how to *observe, profile,* and *track* the enemy, and how to always be the hunter, and never the hunted.

On the Saturday morning after you complete BWT, you'll break camp, grab your gear, and return to *Main Side* to your barracks. Once you settle back into the barracks, your company will form up outside, where you'll run the *Combat Endurance Course* in order to prepare you for next week's Combat Fitness Test. On Sunday, you'll sit through another period of instruction on *Combat Leadership,* and then you'll be "volunteered" to donate blood. Eventually, you'll get a chance to catch a little sleep in order to rest up for the second week of Phase 3.

Phase 3, week two will begin with the Combat Fitness Test. Males and females will perform the same exercises but will be scored differently. The CFT is a training requirement for all recruits, as well as an annual requirement for all Marines. Although the CFT is a type of fitness test, the intent of the CFT is to keep Marines prepared for the physical rigors of today's possible combat scenarios. Accordingly, the CFT is performed while wearing the *Combat Utility* uniform, or *cammies.*

Like the PFT, the CFT is a 300 point test, but rather than calisthenics, an emphasis will be placed on functional fitness needed to meet the demands of combat. It's important that you do well on the CFT because the results will be placed in your *SRB,* or *Service Record Book,* for promotion purposes when you get to the *Fleet Marine Force.*

The Combat Fitness Test can be broken down into three areas:

1. Movement to Contact (MCT)
2. Ammo Can Lift (AL)
3. Maneuver Under Fire (MANUF)

Movement to Contact is an 880-yard sprint. The Ammo Can Lift involves military-pressing a 30-pound ammunition can, fully locking your elbows, for two minutes while earning points for the number of presses done in two minutes. Maneuver Under Fire consists of a 25-yard crawl, hauling a simulated casualty using two different carries over 75 yards through cones, a sprint while carrying two 30-pound ammo cans over 75 yards through the same cones, throwing a dummy hand grenade into a marked circle 22.5 yards away, 3 push-ups, and a sprint with the ammo cans to the finish line.

Third Phase will also be filled with classroom knowledge. One class that I recommend you pay close attention to is *Operational Culture.* As Americans, we often view the world from an *egocentric* perspective, and overlook the fact that values vary greatly among different groups of people, even within the same country or region. We as United States citizens often fail to notice that the needs and motives of human beings differ depending on their particular societies and culture. Oftentimes we assume that an individual or group will respond to an event the way we do simply because that's the way *we* would respond. A correct operational culture mindset, or the proper understanding of a foreign operating environment's collective values system rather than your own perceptions and biases, will be absolutely crucial to mission success.

If recent military history provides any indication of future operations, Marines will continue to work alongside, and operate among, the peoples of Asia, the Middle East, and North Africa. As conflicts in these regions have evolved over the last several years, so too has the Marine Corps' awareness of the need for *operational culture learning*. In response to this awareness, operational culture learning has become central to the way the Marine Corps conducts its *counterinsurgency,* or *COIN,* operations, and many programs have been developed because of that fact. Phase 3 week two's course, *Operational Culture,* will provide you with a foundation for acquiring the *cultural situational awareness* you'll need when deploying to a foreign operating environment.

The third week of Phase Three will begin with two tests—the *Final Written Test* and the *Final PFT.* The Final Written Test will determine what you've learned since the outset of your training. Topics will include Core Values, Ethics, First Aid, and Marine Corps History. BWT subjects such as land navigation and marksmanship will also be covered. The Final PFT will require you to perform the same tasks as the initial PFT, but you'll discover that it won't be as challenging as it was before. This can be attributed to the countless hours of IT that you've been required to perform as an individual and as a unit.

As with Initial Drill, Final Drill will test your platoon's ability to follow orders instantly. There'll be two significant differences between Initial Drill and Final Drill: First, you'll be led in the competition by your Senior Drill Instructor rather than the Junior, and second, your platoon will look like a Marine unit rather than the troupe of clowns it used to be. Each platoon in your company will be evaluated separately, all on the 100-point system, and the platoon with the highest score will win the competition. Both recruits and Drill Instructors will be graded on 25 different drill movements during the competition, including the way the platoon falls into formation.

On Training Day 63, you'll begin the *Crucible*. This event will be a pivotal moment in your career, as well as your life. It will be your *Rite of Passage* to becoming a United States Marine. The Crucible is a 54-hour event that is made up of 12 warrior stations, a day movement course, a day infiltration course, a reaction course, a bayonet assault course, a confidence course, an obstacle course, a team shoot, pugil sticks, a night movement, a night infiltration course, core values classes, hikes, and the Marine Corps Emblem Ceremony. All of these events are designed to promote individual and team confidence, camaraderie, *esprit de corps,* and most importantly—*teamwork.* To facilitate this concept, the Crucible has been designed so that *none of the events can be accomplished alone.*

During the Crucible, your company's platoons will be broken down into squads of approximately 18-20 recruits. Each squad will have a Drill Instructor who will act as its leader, mentor, and advisor. The DI will guide his or her squad and will advise recruits as they negotiate each obstacle. After each event, the DI will debrief his or her recruits.

Throughout the Crucible you'll be allowed roughly four hours of sleep per night. You'll be provided only two and one-half MREs for the entire event. Two MREs will be issued to you at the outset of the event, and a third MRE will be issued to you and another recruit, and the two of you'll have to decide how best to split it among yourselves. The extreme sleep and food deprivation is intended to give you an idea of the stress that you might experience in a combat environment. It's also intended to add to the team-building concept of the Crucible itself.

Successful completion of the Crucible will be mandatory for all recruits. If a recruit fails the Crucible, he or she will be recycled to another company to attempt it again. If a recruit is injured, he or she will be sent to the *Medical Rehabilitation Platoon,* or recommended for discharge, depending upon the severity of the injury.

After the completion of day one and two's events, you'll complete an early morning hike to finish the Crucible on the third day. In a small yet powerful ceremony, you'll be prayed over by a military Chaplain, and then you'll receive the Eagle, Globe, and Anchor Emblem. It's during this ceremony that you'll pass from a recruit to a Marine. If arriving at Phase 2 seemed like euphoria, and if Phase 3 felt like bliss, the completion of the Crucible, which seemingly dissolves your identity as a separate self and transforms you into something far greater, will feel like a *spiritual awakening.* Even if you wanted to, you'll never be able to return to the person you were when you arrived onto the *yellow footprints.*

Keep in mind as you prepare for the Crucible that the level of difficulty of the event has been designed for you to complete it. In other words, the Crucible *is not* designed to "weed out" the weaker recruits from your platoon. Most, if not all, of the inadequately-prepared recruits will have already been recycled to PCP or to following companies in order to bring them up to speed and/or begin their discharge processing.

In contrast, the Crucible was specifically designed to strengthen team bonds and core values. It's demanding for an *individual* Marine to navigate an obstacle or confidence course, but to complete these obstacles as a team with team goals requires much more than physical fitness. For that reason, I highly recommend that you focus solely on leadership traits and don't waste your time trying to analyze the physical aspects of the Crucible. Believe me, you'll have all of the physical stamina you'll need to complete the Crucible from all of the IT that you'll have completed prior to the event. Below are some examples of what I believe you'll need to succeed:

1. **Effective Communication:** In the context of the Crucible, this means being a good listener as well as a talker. You won't

have time to waste when you're trying to communicate with a teammate. This includes both verbal and nonverbal communications. Know that it's well-settled that stress and out-of-control emotions impede effective communication. Before you bark out orders, or respond to them negatively, take a moment to calm down.

2. **Coordination:** During the Crucible, you'll be briefed on each challenge just prior to executing it. That means you'll quickly need to understand the task that needs to be performed, make sure that each team member's role in the task is understood, plan on how your team will execute the task, and do all of this through effective communication. Fortunately, your Drill Instructors will have already appointed a "Team Leader," and you won't have to waste time figuring out whose plan to use.

3. **Cooperation:** Motivate yourself and your team members to stay focused on the *team* goals. Remind your team members that they've been placed on the team to

assist in making the team successful, and that the Marine Corps discourages *individualism.* Celebrate your accomplishments as a team and recognize your teammates for their contributions toward those accomplishments. If teammates happen to make no contributions, don't "muddy the water" with negative criticism. Offer encouraging words anyway.

4. **Adaptability:** Be like the water that takes the shape of the pitcher in which it's poured. Adaptability is the ability to detect changes in your environment and conform to those changes in order to complete a task, even if it takes you out of your comfort zone. Good adaptability has been linked to good situational awareness.

5. **Team Spirit:** Motivate your team to be willing to work together with loyalty and enthusiasm. Make positive statements to keep the team motivated. If you see other members of the team experiencing difficulty with a task, instead of raising your voice and correcting them, help

them. If one of your teammates loses an MRE, give them yours.

Once you receive your Eagle, Globe, and Anchor, you'll be marched to the chow hall, where you'll be rewarded for your accomplishment with the *Warrior's Breakfast.* This will be the first meal in eleven weeks where you'll get to eat all you want of what you want, and talk while doing it. Not only will you be able to talk with your fellow Marines, but you'll also have an opportunity to communicate with your Drill Instructors outside of the DI-Recruit relationship. Remember to moderate your food intake because you won't be used to that much food. Just as well, don't get too loose with your Drill Instructors because until you graduate, they're still your Drill Instructors and are *not* your buddies.

The *Crucible* will end on Saturday of Training Week 11. The next day you'll be granted an on-base *Liberty.* This means that you'll be allowed to walk around the base in small groups, shop at the *Base Exchange,* or store, eat at one of MCRD's fast-food restaurants, and even call home. It's important to know that you'll be "under the microscope" like never before. One way to get into big trouble is to walk past an Officer and not render a salute. It'll take you a while to recognize an Officer from a distance, especially when he or she is wearing cammies. Some great advice that my DIs gave me was *"when in doubt, whip it out,"* meaning, of course, your salute. It's far better to salute an enlisted Marine than to not salute a Commissioned Officer.

Although you'll "technically" become a Marine when you receive your Emblem, you won't "officially" become a Marine until you're *dismissed* from Recruit Training on Graduation Day. This means that, once you finish your Warrior's Breakfast, until the time you'll graduate, you'll still have plenty to accomplish. This includes completing your final week of Marine Recruit Training.

Your final week of Recruit Training is known as *Marine Week.* This week will include your *Battalion Commander's Inspection, Family Day,* and *Graduation.*

Marine Week is a type of "decompression," that allows you to shed the recruit behaviors that no longer befit a United States Marine. An example of a recruit behavior would be referring to yourself in the third person, as you've been required to do since day one.

The *Battalion Commander's Inspection,* a mandatory graduation requirement, will be an opportunity for your Battalion Commander to ensure that recruits are upholding the high standards of the Marine Corps. It's also intended to familiarize you with interacting confidently with high-grade Officers. During the inspection, the Commander will inspect your uniform, weapon, knowledge, and *military bearing.* Once the Battalion Commander gives his final approval, *then and only then* will you be considered ready to graduate. Don't get cocky just because you've completed the Crucible and received your Eagle, Globe, and Anchor. You're Battalion Commander can take it from you much easier than it took you to earn it.

Family Day will require you to run a mandatory *Motivational Run,* afford you an opportunity to practice for your *Graduation Ceremony,* and allow you an opportunity to spend time with family and friends. Like liberty before, it'll be especially important for you to carry yourself as a Marine while out and about. It's also crucial that you avoid the "off-limits" areas of MCRD.

During *Family Day,* I was so motivated, that even though I had seven family members present, I chose to spend family time at the base gym hitting chest and triceps with my Drill Instructor. That may sound crazy, but to me it was (and always will be) one of the greatest honors I've ever experience.

The final day of Phase 3 is the day you've been waiting for—*Graduation Day.* The *Morning Colors Ceremony,* with musical accompaniment by the Depot's *Marine Band,* will begin at 0745 in front of the Commanding General's building. At 0900, the *Graduation Ceremony* will begin on the *Parade Deck,* where the bleachers will be filled with hundreds of parents, family, and friends. The Ceremony will last about an hour, and include distinguished guests such as the Commanding General of MCRD. At the end of the ceremony, you'll hear the word "Dismissed." Once dismissed, you'll be congratulated by your Drill Instructors, and will, from that point forward, forever be able to claim the title, *United States Marine.*

After you've graduated, you'll be given a brief 10-day leave period before your next challenge, *Marine Combat Training (MCT).* During this ten days, you may be selected to work as a *Recruiter's Assistant* at your hometown Recruiting Station. During Recruiter's Assistance, you'll spend time helping Recruiters interview potential Marine prospects, and share your experiences with those prospects. Once your leave expires, you'll report as ordered to the Marine Corps' *School of Infantry (SOI)* for MCT, where you'll experience first-hand why every Marine, regardless of his or her MOS, is a combat-ready Rifleman. Maintain your physical fitness while on leave. You'll need it once you report to MCT.

After successful completion of MCT, you'll travel to your job-specific school, where you'll receive your specialty training. Once you've completed your specialty training and receive an MOS, you'll be assigned to your *Permanent Duty Station,* where you'll finally begin your career as a member of "The World's Finest Fighting Force." Good luck, and *Semper fi!*

Glossary I-Acronyms and Abbreviations

ACE—aviation combat element

C2—command and control

CE—command element

CMC—Commandant of the Marine Corps

DOTMLPF—doctrine, organization, training, materiel, leadership and education, personnel, and facilities

GCE—ground combat element

GDF—Guidance for the Development of the Force

GEF—Guidance for the Employment of the Force

ISR—intelligence, surveillance, and reconnaissance

JPG—Joint Planning Guidance

JSCP—Joint Strategic Capabilities Plan

LCE—logistics combat element

MAGTF—Marine air-ground task force

MARSOC—United States Marine Corps Forces, Special Operations Command

MCLC—Marine Corps Logistics Command

MEB—Marine expeditionary brigade

MEF—Marine expeditionary force

MEU—Marine expeditionary unit

MIO—maritime interception operations

MOS—military occupational specialty

MPF(F)—maritime prepositioning force (future)

NCO—noncommissioned officer

OSD—Office of the Secretary of Defense

PME—professional military education

SPMAGTF—special purpose Marine air-ground task force

STOVL—short take-off and vertical landing aircraft

UAS—unmanned aircraft system

UCP—Unified Command Plan

USAFRICOM—United States Africa Command

USCENTCOM—United States Central Command

USJFCOM—United States Joint Forces Command

USSOCOM—United States Special Operations Command

Glossary II-Terms and Definitions

amphibious shipping—Organic Navy ships specifically designed to transport, land, and support landing forces in amphibious assault operations and capable of being loaded or unloaded by naval personnel without external assistance in the amphibious objective area. (JP 1-02)

antiair warfare—That action required to destroy or reduce to an acceptable level the enemy air and missile threat. Antiair warfare integrates all offensive and defensive actions against enemy aircraft, surface-to-air weapons, and theater missiles into a singular, indivisible set of operations. It is one of the six functions of Marine aviation. Also called AAW. (MCRP 5-12C)

assault echelon—In amphibious operations, the element of a force comprised of tailored units and aircraft assigned to conduct the initial assault on the operational area. (JP 1-02)

assault follow-on echelon—In amphibious operations, that echelon of the assault troops, vehicles, aircraft, equipment, and supplies that, though not needed to initiate the assault, is required to support and sustain the assault. In order to accomplish its purpose, it is normally required in the objective area no later than five days after commencement of the assault landing. Also called AFOE. (JP 1-02)

assault support—The use of aircraft to provide tactical mobility and logistic support for the Marine air-ground task force, the movement of high priority cargo and personnel within the immediate area of operations, in-flight refueling, and the evacuation of personnel and cargo. Assault support is one of the functions of Marine aviation. (MCRP 5-12C)

aviation combat element—The core element of a Marine air-ground task force (MAGTF) that is task-organized to conduct aviation operations. The aviation combat element (ACE) provides all or a portion of the six functions of Marine aviation necessary to accomplish the MAGTF's mission. These functions are antiair warfare, offensive air support, assault support, electronic warfare, air reconnaissance, and control of aircraft and missiles. The ACE is usually composed of an aviation unit headquarters and various other aviation units or their detachments. It can vary in size from a small aviation detachment of specifically required aircraft to one or more Marine aircraft wings. In a joint or multinational environment, the ACE may contain other Service or multinational forces assigned or attached to the MAGTF. The ACE itself is not a formal command. Also called ACE. (MCRP 5-12C)

battlespace—All aspects of air, surface, subsurface, land, space, and electromagnetic spectrum that encompass the area of influence and area of interest. (MCRP 5-12C)

civil-military operations—The activities of a commander that establish, maintain, influence, or exploit relations between military forces, governmental and nongovernmental civilian organizations and authorities, and the civilian populace in a friendly, neutral, or hostile operational area in order to facilitate military operations, to consolidate and achieve operational US objectives. Civil-military operations may include performance by military forces of activities and functions normally the responsibility of the local, regional, or national government. These activities may occur prior to, during, or subsequent to other military actions. They may also occur, if directed, in the absence of other military operations. Civil-military operations may be performed by designated civil affairs, by other military forces, or by a combination of civil affairs and other forces. Also called CMO. (JP 1-02)

combatant command—A unified or specified command with a broad continuing mission under a single commander established and so designated by the President, through the Secretary of Defense and with the advice and assistance of the Chairman of the Joint Chiefs of Staff. Combatant commands typically have geographical or functional responsibilities. (JP 1-02)

combatant commander—A commander of one of the unified or specified combatant commands established by the President. Also called CCDR. (JP 1-02)

combat power—The total means of destructive and/or disruptive force which a military unit/formation can apply against the opponent at a given time. (JP 1-02)

command element—The core element of a Marine air-ground task force (MAGTF) that is the headquarters. The command element (CE) is composed of the commander, general or executive and special staff sections, headquarters section, and requisite communications support, intelligence, and reconnaissance forces, necessary to accomplish the MAGTF's mission. The CE provides command and control, intelligence, and other support essential for effective planning and execution of operations by the other elements of the MAGTF. The CE varies in size and composition; and, in a joint or multinational environment, it may contain other Service or multinational forces assigned or attached to the MAGTF. Also called CE. (MCRP 5-12C)

control of aircraft and missiles—The coordinated employment of facilities, equipment, communications, procedures, and personnel that allows the aviation combat element (ACE) commander to plan, direct, and control the efforts of the ACE to support the accomplishment of the Marine air-ground task force mission. Control of aircraft and missiles is one of the six functions of Marine aviation. (MCRP 5-12C)

conventional forces—1. Those forces capable of conducting operations using non-nuclear weapons. 2. Those forces other than designated special operations forces. (JP 1-02)

counterinsurgency—Those military, paramilitary, political, economic, psychological, and civic actions taken by a government to defeat insurgency. Also called COIN. (JP 1-02)

crisis—An incident or situation involving a threat to a nation, its territories, citizens, military forces, possessions, or vital interests that develops rapidly and creates a condition of such diplomatic, economic, political, or military importance that commitment of military forces and resources is contemplated to achieve national objectives. (JP 1-02)

electronic warfare—Military action involving the use of electromagnetic and directed energy to control the electromagnetic spectrum or to attach the enemy. Electronic warfare consists of three divisions: electronic attack, electronic protection, and electronic warfare support. Also called EW. (JP 1-02)

expeditionary force—An armed force organized to accomplish a specific objective in a foreign country. (JP 1-02)

forcible entry—Seizing and holding of a military lodgment in the face of armed opposition. See also lodgment. (JP 1-02)

ground combat element—The core element of a Marine air-ground task force (MAGTF) that is task-organized to conduct ground operations. It is usually constructed around an infantry organization but can vary in size from a small ground unit of any type to one or more Marine divisions that can be independently maneuvered under the direction of the MAGTF commander. It includes appropriate ground combat and combat support forces, and in a joint or multinational environment, it may also contain other Service or multinational forces assigned or attached to the MAGTF. The ground combat element itself is not a formal command. Also called GCE. (MCRP 5-12C)

instrument of national power—All the means available to the government in its pursuit of national objectives. They are expressed as diplomatic, economic, informational and military. (JP 1-02)

intelligence, surveillance, and reconnaissance—An activity that synchronizes and integrates the planning and operation sensors, assets, and processing, exploitation, and dissemination systems in direct support of current and future operations. This is an integrated intelligence and operations function. Also called ISR. (JP 1-02)

interagency—United States Government agencies and departments, including the Department of Defense. See also interagency coordination. (JP 1-02)

irregular challenges—Challenges posed by those employing unconventional methods to counter the traditional advantages of stronger opponents. (NDS)

irregular warfare—A violent struggle among state and non-state actors for legitimacy and influence over the relevant population(s). Irregular warfare favors indirect and asymmetric approaches, though it may employ the full range of military and other capacities, in order to erode an adversary's power, influence, and will. Also called IW. (JP 1-02)

joint—Connotes activities, operations, organizations, etc., in which elements of two or more Military Departments participate. (JP 1-02)

joint force—A general term applied to a force composed of significant elements, assigned or attached, of two or more Military Departments operating under a single joint force commander. See also join force commander. (JP 1-02)

littoral—The littoral comprises two segments of battlespace: 1. Seaward: the area from the open ocean to the shore, which must be controlled to support operations ashore. 2. Landward: the area inland from the shore that can be supported and defended directly from the sea. (JP 1-02)

logistics combat element—The core element of a Marine air-ground task force (MAGTF) that is task-organized to provide the combat service support necessary to accomplish the MAGTF's mission. The logistics combat element varies in size from a small detachment to one or more Marine logistics groups. It provides supply, maintenance, transportation, general engineering, health services, and a variety of other multinational forces assigned or attached to the MAGTF. The logistics combat element itself is not a formal command. Also called LCE. (MCRP 5-12C)

maneuver—1. A movement to place ships, aircraft, or land forces in a position of advantage over the enemy. 2. A tactical exercise carried out at sea, in the air, on the ground, or on a map in imitation of war. 3. The operation of a ship, aircraft, or vehicle, to cause it to perform desired movements. 4. Employment of forces in the operational area through movement in combination with fires to achieve a position of advantage in respect to the enemy in order to accomplish the mission. (JP 1-02)

maneuver warfare—A warfighting philosophy that seeks to shatter the enemy's cohesion through a variety of rapid, focused, and unexpected actions that create a turbulent and rapidly deteriorating situation with which the enemy cannot cope. (MCRP 5-12C)

Marine air-ground task force—The Marine Corps' principle organization for all missions across the range of military operations, composed of forces task-organized under a single commander capable of responding rapidly to a contingency anywhere in the world. The types of forces in the Marine air-ground task force (MAGTF) are functionally grouped into four core elements: a command element, an aviation combat element, a ground combat element, and a logistics combat element. The four core elements are categories of forces, not formal commands. The basic structure of the MAGTF never varies, though the number, size, and type of Marine Corps units comprising each of its four elements will always be mission dependent. The flexibility of the organizational structure allows for one or more subordinate MAGTFs to be assigned. In a joint or multinational environment, other Service or multinational forces may be assigned or attached. Also called MAGTF. (MCRP 5-12C)

Marine aviation functions—The six functions (antiair warfare, offensive air support, assault support, electronic warfare, air reconnaissance, and control of aircraft and missiles) performed by Marine aviation in support of the Marine air-ground task force. (MCRP 5-12C)

Marine expeditionary brigade—Marine air-ground task force (MAGTF) that is constructed around a reinforced infantry regiment, a composite Marine aircraft group, and a combat logistics regiment. The Marine expeditionary brigade (MEB), commanded by a general officer, is task-organized to meet the requirements of a specific situation. It can function as part of a joint task force, as the lead echelon of the Marine expeditionary force (MEF), or alone. It varies in size and composition and is larger than a Marine expeditionary unit but smaller than a MEF. The MEB is capable of conducting missions across the full range of military operations. In a joint or multinational environment, it may also contain other Service or multinational forces assigned or attached to the MAGTF. Also called MEB. (MCRP 5-12C)

Marine expeditionary force—The largest Marine air-ground task force (MAGTF) and the Marine Corps' principle warfighting organization, particularly for larger crises or contingencies. It is task-organized around permanent command element and normally contains one or more Marine divisions, Marine aircraft wings, and Marine logistics groups. The Marine expeditionary force is capable of missions across the range of military operations, including amphibious assault and sustained operations ashore in any environment. It can operate from a sea base, a land base, or both. In a joint or multinational environment, it may also contain other Service or multinational forces assigned or attached to the MAGTF. Also called MEF. (MCRP 5-12C)

Marine expeditionary unit—A Marine air-ground task force (MAGTF) that is constructed around an infantry battalion reinforced, a helicopter squadron reinforced, and a task-organized logistics combat element. It normally fulfills Marine Corps' forward sea-based deployment requirements. The Marine expeditionary unit provides an immediate reaction capability for crisis response and is capable of limited combat operations. In a joint or multinational environment, it may contain other Service or multinational forces assigned or attached to the MAGTF. Also called MEU. (MCRP 5-12C)

maritime interception operations—Efforts to monitor, query, and board merchant vessels in international waters to enforce sanctions against other nations such as those in support of United Nations Security Council Resolutions and/or prevent the transport of restricted goods. Also called MIO. (JP 1-02)

maritime prepositioning force—A task organization of units under one commander formed for the purpose of introducing a Marine air-ground task force (MAGTF) and its associated equipment and supplies into a secure area. The maritime prepositioning force is composed of a command element, a maritime prepositioning ships squadron, a MAGTF, and a Navy support element. Also called MPF. (MCRP 5-12C)

multicapable—Operationally decisive across the range of military operations with a capacity tailored to combatant commanders' requirements; optimized to operate as an integrated system through the air, land, and maritime domains. (Proposed for inclusion in the next edition of MCRP 5-12C)

multinational—Between two or more forces or agencies of two or more nations or coalition partners. (JP 1-02)

multinational force—A force composed of military elements of nations who have formed an alliance or coalition for some specific purpose. Also called MNF. (JP 1-02)

noncombatant evacuation operations—Operations directed by the Department of State or other appropriate authority, in conjunction with the Department of Defense, whereby noncombatants are evacuated from foreign countries when their lives are endangered by war, civil unrest, or natural disaster to safe havens or to the United States. Also called NEOs. (JP 1-02)

nongovernmental organization—A private, self-governing, not-for-profit organization dedicated to alleviating human suffering; and/or promoting education, health care, economic development, environmental protection, human rights, and conflict resolution; and/or encouraging the establishment of democratic institutions and civil society. Also called NGO. (JP 1-02)

offensive air support—Those air operations conducted against enemy installations, facilities, and personnel to directly assist the attainment of MAGTF objectives by the destruction of enemy resources or the isolation of the enemy's military forces. Offensive air support is one of the six functions of Marine aviation. Also called OAS. (MCRP 5-12C)

overseas—All locations, including Alaska and Hawaii, outside the continental United States. (JP 1-02)

professional military education—The systematic instruction of professionals in subjects that will enhance their knowledge of the science and art of war. Also called PME. (MCRP 5-12C)

sea base—An inherently maneuverable, scalable aggregation of distributed, networked platforms that enables the global power projection of offensive and defensive forces from the sea and includes the ability to assemble, equip, project, support, and sustain those forces without reliance on land bases within the joint operations area. (NTRP 1-02)

seabasing—A national capability and overarching transformational operating concept for projecting and sustaining naval power and joint forces, which assures joint access by leveraging the operational maneuver of sovereign, distributed, and networked forces operating globally from the sea. (MCRP 5-12C)

security cooperation—All Department of Defense interactions with foreign defense establishments to build defense relationships that promote specific US security interests, develop allied and friendly military capabilities for self-defense and multinational operations, and provide US forces with peacetime and contingency access to a host nation. (JP 1-02)

security cooperation activity—Military activity that involves other nations and is intended to shape the operational environment in peacetime. Activities include programs and exercises that the US military conducts with other nations to improve mutual understanding and improve interoperability with treaty partners or potential coalition partners. They are designed to support a combatant commander's theater strategy as articulated in the theater security cooperation plan. (JP 1-02)

supporting establishment—Those personnel, bases, and activities that support the Marine Corps operating forces. (Excerpt from MCDP 1-0)

terrorism—The calculated use of unlawful violence or threat of unlawful violence to inculcate fear; intended to coerce or to intimidate government or societies in the pursuit of goals that are generally political, religious, or ideological. (JP 1-02)

weapons of mass destruction—Weapons that are capable of a high order of destruction and/or of being used in such a manner as to destroy large numbers of people. Weapons of mass destruction can be high-yield explosives or nuclear, biological, chemical, or radiological weapons, but exclude the means of transporting or propelling the weapon where such means is a separable and divisible part of the weapon. Also called WMD. (JP 1-02)

Glossary References

Joint Publication 1-02, Department of Defense Dictionary of Military and Associated Terms (Washington DC, Department of Defense, 12 April 2001)

Marine Corps Doctrinal Publication 1, Warfighting, (Washington DC: United States Marine Corps, June 1997)

Marine Corps Doctrinal Publication 1-0, Marine Corps Operations, (Washington DC: United States Marine Corps, Sept 2001)

Marine Corps Reference Publication 5-12C, Marine Corps Supplement to the Department of Defense Dictionary of Military and Associated Terms, (Washington DC: United States Marine Corps, July 1998)

National Defense Strategy of the United States, (Washington DC: Department of Defense, March 1, 2005)

Navy Tactical Reference Publication 1-02, Navy Supplement to the Department of Defense Dictionary of Military and Associated Terms (Washington DC: United States Navy, August 2006)

Navy Warfighting Publication 4-01, Naval Transportation, (Washington DC: United States Navy, May 2007)